MOVING *THROUGH* LOSS

MOVING *THROUGH* LOSS

By

Christine Lalli Bavaro, LMHC

With

Anne Elise O'Connor

iUniverse, Inc.
New York   Bloomington

Moving *Through* Loss

iUniverse books may be ordered through booksellers or by contacting:

iUniverse
1663 Liberty Drive
Bloomington, IN 47403
www.iuniverse.com
1-800-Authors (1-800-288-4677)

Because of the dynamic nature of the Internet, any Web addresses or links contained in this book may have changed since publication and may no longer be valid. The views expressed in this work are solely those of the author and do not necessarily reflect the views of the publisher, and the publisher hereby disclaims any responsibility for them.

ISBN: 978-0-595-53446-3 (pbk)
ISBN: 978-0-595-63504-7 (ebk)

Printed in the United States of America

iUniverse rev. date: 3/6/2009

To family and friends who have helped me,
To Divine Wisdom who inspired me,
To Wally who made me happy,
Thank you

CONTENTS

Acknowledgments 1

I. View from the Balcony. 5
   Emergency Flower Essences 12
   Soothing Flower Essences 13

II. When Tragedy Strikes. 15
   Helpful Hints for Surviving 18
   Worksheet I: Reaction 19

III. Our Life Together 21
   "Chrysalis of Sleep" by Marcia Molay 22
   Helpful Hints for Remembering. 28
   Worksheet II: Remembering. 29

IV. The Journey Begins. 31
   "Out of the Depths" by Marsie Silvestro 32
   Helpful Hints for Self-Nurturance 41
   Worksheet III: Consoling Ourselves 43

V. Uncharted Territory. 45
   Poetry by Elizabeth Kübler-Ross. 46
   Helpful Hints for Reconnection 56
   Worksheet IV: Finding Our Way 57

VI. Pack Up Your Sorrows 59
   "New Relationship" by Marcia Molay. 60
   Helpful Hints for Change. 65
   Worksheet V: Changes 67

VII. From the Balcony to Center Stage. 69
   "Allowing" by CLB. 70
   Helpful Hints for Self-Discovery 76
   Worksheet VI: Discovering 77

VIII. Signals from the Beyond 79
    "I Am Not Alone" by CLB 80
    Worksheet VII: Messages? 84

Epilogue 85

Resources 87

Bibliography 89

About the Authors 91

Acknowledgments

Many influences came into play in the writing of this book. First, there was the decision to share my story with others. Going public with something so personal took a giant leap of faith. Once that was resolved, there was the frustration that in spite of my well-intended decision, I knew I needed help to link it all together. For that, I turned to the expertise of Anne Elise O'Connor, who provided invaluable guidance. She took my raw, emotional journal entries and helped translate my experience into something others might find readable. Anne Elise helped me organize my thoughts and kept urging me to remember things I wanted to forget. I am grateful for her patience and her friendship. I doubt I would have brought this book into the light without her help.

David Dalton, my flower essence teacher and friend, was the first to tell me, "You will be writing a book about this." He planted the seed for my decision to tell others how flower essences helped bring solace in my experience of loss, grief, and recovery. I am so grateful to David for his insight and encouragement. He is a gifted teacher. I am fortunate and privileged to learn from him.

A major influence in my learning has been Chonyi Richard Allen, a friend and teacher of the Personal Totem Pole Process and Native American and Buddhist studies. He taught me about inner journeying and the value of "allowing." The journeys shared here come from my work with Richard during and after my husband's illness. I appreciate the opportunity to continue to learn from him. The clarity and sensitivity of his work is reflected in the authenticity of his being.

Acquaintances, clients, friends, and family, each in their own way, have influenced my thoughts and understanding of life's passages. I have been blessed with many friends whose support has helped me feel loved and protected. A loving thank you to Karen Wilk, Roberta and Mario Tortorici, Marie and Joe Bogan, Rita Meyers, Pat and Ed Baker, Bob and Chee-Chee DiGiammarino, Ellie and Frank Adorn, and Pat and Charlie Byrne for your company, advice, and *handyman help*. Your love for Wally was evident in your thoughtfulness toward me.

I extend a special thank you to my Healer's Group: Marsie Silvestro, Robin Anasazi, Diane Grant, and Pat Huxley-Cohen. We are all in human services and meet regularly to discuss the gifts of Spirit and how they influence our work. Truly, your encouragement, wise advice, and good nature kept me afloat during this writing process. You, individually and collectively, listened, made suggestions, corrected my sentences, and said all of the right things to help me bring this book to fruition.

To Marcia Molay and Marsie Silvestro, who have generously allowed me to include their heartfelt poetry, a very special thank you. Your writings touch the soul and heal the heart.

To my children, who have fulfilled their father's instruction to "take care of your mother," you make it possible for me to share my story with others. Simply, I love you.

For your prayers and support, many thanks to my brother-in-law, Father John. You were a wonderful shoulder to lean on for all of us.

In many families, it seems that one or two relatives become real friends. For me, my sister's daughter, my niece, Joanne, is that person. Our weekly long-distance conversations were, and still are, such a source of love and comfort. I know my sister smiles down upon us.

And finally, but not least, to my precious grandchildren, you have been a ray of light—Papa would be proud!

Chapter I
View from the Balcony

I moved into the very last row of the very last balcony in this strange theatre as I experienced the illness and death of my husband of forty-three years. I'm not quite sure when I took up residence there, but while living in the balcony, I watched myself attend to the business of daily living, doing what had to be done and feeling only enough to know that I still had a toehold on the reality of my existence.

Between birth and death, we move through our daily lives somewhat unconsciously, noticing only those things that are of immediate concern to us. When we are confronted by a profound event, something that rocks—if not demolishes—our very foundation, we are forced to consciously make meaning of every part of our lives. Anything that changes "life as we know it," such as birth, illness, job loss, or financial loss, makes us stop, regroup, and, if we are lucky, move forward. However, when that profound event is a life-threatening diagnosis, the possibility of "no tomorrow" thrusts us into a sea of fear and despair, the depths of which are endless. We struggle to keep our hope alive, but all too often, reality does not support our effort. We then learn to live in the "in-between" of life and death, cherishing every moment and hating it at the same time.

How we grapple with the "in-between" is the most personal of journeys, yet it is also the most universal. Although the ending is always the same, the moving on is different for all. Every loss leaves the survivor with profound questions, unique to the relationship, to ponder. When your spouse dies, you are not just grieving the loss of that person, you are grieving the loss of a lifestyle you built together and your definition of who you are. *How* you will live without that person is not the only question to be answered. Ultimately, one must ask, "Who am I?"

This book is about my experience during my husband's illness, his death, and my recovery. Throughout this journey, I wrote about my thoughts and feelings, hoping the words would help me understand and survive my emotional pain. As the experience of this devastating loss unfolded, I discovered my journey through grief had led me on a path of self-discovery.

I have been a family systems therapist and mental health counselor for more than thirty years. I have had the privilege of counseling children, families, widows, and widowers, struggling to make their life whole again after suffering a profound loss. I am not unfamiliar with the impact that the death of a loved one has on those who survive. However, I am always amazed at the intensity of feeling and the fact that we actually recover. Having walked this path with death "up close and personal," I am impressed with our resiliency, yours and mine, which allows us to laugh again.

From childhood, my sister and I lived with the expectation that my father would be dying, practically any day, according to my mother. It's one of those quirky family patterns that are too complicated to explain here, except to say that my father died at ninety-six, basically from old age, in January 1989. Actually, 1989 was a busy year for dying in my family because in April, my mother-in-law passed away from cancer, and then my mother topped off the year by dying on Christmas Day after ten days in a coma that resulted from a fall.

Each loss leaves its own mark on the survivor. It's common knowledge that upon the loss of the parents, we consider the child an orphan. In 1989, I was surprised that I, a grown woman with a family of her own, also felt like an orphan. My reaction to my parents dying was the driving force that led me to explore death, dying, and survivor recovery. I wrapped myself in bereavement courses and conferences that introduced me to the philosophy and psychology of many leaders in the field. After digesting my newfound academic knowledge and integrating it with my own experiences, I passed my insights along to others in workshops where participants shared their experiences, confirming what I had learned. I folded this newly acquired information into my psychotherapy practice, which is grounded in traditional cognitive-behavioral and family systems theory.

In 2001, the mark left by the loss of my sister required more of an internal search to gain understanding about what it was like living without her and without a family of origin. I felt this to be a different type of loss than that of my parents. It was a loss that led me to think about my own mortality. Previously trained in working with hypnotherapy and imagery, I started using these therapeutic modalities to help process my new feelings. Both therapeutic models require the process of deep relaxation, during which a conversation emerges with the spontaneous images that arise from the unconscious. These images act as a barometer for your feelings and are a gentle way of exploring painful emotions. I found working in this modality informative and soothing.

Flower Essences

A few months before my husband was diagnosed, while I was still grieving the loss of my sister, a friend told me about flower essences. I responded, "What are flower essences?" And with that question, I began my ongoing exploration of flower essences. I discovered that flower essences are plant energy or liquid remedies made from fresh flowers. Safe, gentle, and without any known side effects, they belong to a family of natural remedies referred to as vibrational medicine. More familiar examples of vibrational medicine are homeopathy, acupuncture, and Reiki. Richard Gerber, MD, writes, *"Vibrational medicine is a healing approach which is based upon the Einsteinian concept of matter as energy, and of human beings as a series of complex energy fields in dynamic equilibrium."* Flower essences can bring balance to our energy fields which aids us in moving through our loss.

Flower essences were first brought to general attention through the work of Edward Bach, MD, of England (1886–1936). An immunologist and bacteriologist, Dr. Bach was a traditional physician practicing in London. He was also a researcher, who discovered a number of bacteria in the gastrointestinal tract associated with various illnesses and developed vaccines to treat those illnesses. Over the years, his research convinced him that there was a connection between illness and emotions—a concept that is widely accepted today.

In the early days of medicine, people looked to nature for healing agents to meet their patients' needs. When Dr. Bach's own illness required a move to the countryside, he became increasingly interested in the healing properties of plants, trees, and flowers. Dr. Bach determined that morning dew on flowers held the healing vibrational essence of the flower. He treated himself, as well as his patients, with these essences. In this way, Dr. Bach learned from personal experience as well as from the information derived from his patients.

As people began to experience relief of their symptoms, flower essences became increasingly popular. Dr. Bach created a way to replicate the morning dew by soaking the flower in a bowl of sunlit spring water placed near the plant. The energy of the flower was then absorbed into the water. Modern practitioners continue to make flower essences as Dr. Bach taught. By 1930, Dr. Bach had developed a holistic system of healing that was grounded in the empirical evidence gathered through his case studies using these gifts from nature. In 1981, the Food and Drug Administration approved the Bach Flower Essences as a form of homeopathy.

The description of each essence identifies the physical, personality, and behavioral characteristics that the essence helps. They are sold in a dropper bottle. Taking as few as two to four drops under the tongue or on the wrist, once to four times a day, can bring balance to your system allowing you to help yourself move forward. Some essences can be found in health food stores and come with instructions on how to self-administer. Others are available through certified practitioners. Many practitioners throughout the world have carried Dr. Bach's work forward, and hundreds of other essences have been discovered. In addition to Delta Gardens of New Hampshire, where I received my certification, there are other sources including the Flower Essence Society in California, Woodland Essences in New York, and many more too numerous to mention here; many have established training programs. I have also completed level two of the Bach International Education Program.

Inner Journeys

Throughout the book, I have included some of the journeys experienced during my *moving through loss*. Journeys begin with allowing oneself to become deeply relaxed with the aid of music or induction from an imagery guide or hypnotherapist. Most people are familiar with hypnosis or guided imagery, best known for helping with unwanted habits such as smoking or overeating, for relaxation, and for desensitizing people to fears of flying or elevators. The use of imagination in therapy is commonly experienced through guided imagery.

I once saw a billboard overlooking the highway that quoted Einstein: "Whatever can be imagined can be achieved." The unconscious speaks to us through the imagination, through dreams, and through bodily feelings and sensations. I think the title of Belleruth Naparstek's book *Staying Well with Guided Imagery: How to Harness the Power of Your Imagination for Health and Healing* says it all. During the grief time, our senses are working overtime to protect and guide us through the overwhelming and unwanted reality of our loss.

Along with guided imagery there is also a technique called active imagination, which was developed by the noted psychiatrist,

C. G. Jung (1875–1961). Usually accessed while deeply relaxed, the process of active imagination creates an internal conversation that helps the individual resolve past or present feelings. Jungian psychologist and professor Verena Kast writes about Jung's active imagination technique in her book *Imagination As Space of Freedom: Dialogue Between the Ego and the Unconscious*—an informative account about the use of active imagination and the healing experience in psychotherapy.

While studying hypnotherapy and guided imagery, I came upon a very creative therapy model, The Personal Totem Pole Process created by E. Stephen Gallegos, PhD, of New Mexico. With influences from Native American folklore, it draws upon spontaneous imagery, often in the form of animals, which the journeyer dialogues with as their inner wisdom unfolds from the energy centers of the body. In 1993, I completed a three-year intensive training program led by Chonyi Richard Allen, M.Ed., who is fluent in the ancient traditions of Eastern Cherokee and Buddhist studies; Barbara Smith, LICSW; Margaret Vasington, LICSW; and E. Stephen Gallegos, PhD. The Personal Totem Pole Process is also a form of therapy that one can do on one's own with a CD or with the help of a trained professional, which I would recommend.

Mind/Body Medicine, heralded by Herbert Benson, MD, has taught us that when we experience stress, the autonomic nervous system does not distinguish bad stress from good stress. Be it a wedding or a wake, the body has an automatic response. The grief time is so stressful that it is extremely important to pay attention to our physical, as well as our emotional, health. The body's ability to heal itself through imagery is a resource not to be overlooked when recovering from grief. Imagery, whether guided or active, is a process of allowing, not doing. When we relax the body, engaging all of our senses, we relax the mind, allowing our inner wisdom to reveal our deepest feelings in the language of symbols. It is a gentler way to process our sorrow. Our knowing is the gift of trusting our feelings, our senses, and our imagery, as well as our thinking.

My purpose in writing this book is to let others know of the valuable contribution of complementary therapies. Based on personal experience, I believe them to be a useful adjunct to psychotherapy and especially helpful when experiencing grief. Many people dismiss them as "New Age woo-woo." I can understand that, as I was once one of those people. Not anymore. I have witnessed how helpful they have been to others … and to me. Flower essences brought an enormous level of comfort to me and, through me, to my husband as well. We were able to keep the despair of the reality at a reasonable distance, allowing us to make the most of every day.

In addition to the flower essences and inner journeys that are mentioned throughout the story, I have included information on the stages of healing. Each chapter offers simple, effective, and helpful hints for coping, suggestions that worked for me and some that I wish I had thought of during my ordeal.

Writing from the heart is a well-known therapeutic tool that costs you nothing but time and gives back to you priceless comfort and clarity if you allow yourself a little consistency of putting pen to paper—or I should say, fingers to keyboard. I have included worksheets with questions to consider so that you may write about your experience of *moving through loss*. The questions touch upon areas we would prefer to forget, but that live on in the deep recesses of our hearts, only to be activated again whenever there is a reminder—a moment that presents itself when you look up and see a person who is wearing a jacket similar to the one he had or when the song on the store's speaker system is the song that you danced to once upon a time. Writing from the heart is a healing process.

As you move through your loss, I hope my journey from the balcony to center stage encourages you to seek whatever form of therapeutic intervention feels right for you.

Christine L. Bavaro, M.Ed., LMHC
Danvers, Massachusetts

Emergency Essences

When crisis strikes, and particularly in the early days of mourning, two of the most helpful flower essence blends are:

°Rescue Remedy by Bach

Rock Rose ... restores courage and peace of mind.
Star of Bethlehem ... neutralizes the trauma of receiving bad news; restores inner peace.
Impatiens ... calms when you are feeling impatient, irritable, tense, or frustrated.
Cherry Plum ... restores balance when you feel like you're about to lose control.
Clematis ... keeps you focused when you are having difficulty concentrating.

°Emergency Protection Blend by Delta Gardens

Angelica ... assists when one is going through rapid change.
Cinquefoil ... cleanses the energy field.
Pennyroyal ... protects recycling of thoughts and protects from obsessions.
Rue ... repels negative energies directed toward one by others.
St. John's Wort ... seals and strengthens the energy field.
Yarrow ... strengthens the energy field to repel others' negativity.

Soothing Essences

During times of sadness and pain, we look for something that soothes, calms, and heals our wounds. As children, we found hot chocolate and cookies comforting; as adults, we look to our family and friends for help. When that help is not enough, we can turn to flower essences to gently nurture us back to health.

The following essences from Bach, Delta Gardens, and the Flower Essence Society are among the many that comfort.

Star of Bethlehem ... restores inner peace and neutralizes trauma.
Mariposa Lily ... is for nurturance.
Lemon Balm ... allows for deeper relaxation.
Mimulus ... quiets known fears.
Sweet Chestnut ... eases mental anguish.
Red Chestnut ... eases overconcern for others.

Chapter II

When Tragedy Strikes

February 26, 2002

… back from the sunny South … the flight home was uneventful … to keep myself busy, I made a mental list of all the good I have in my life. After three weeks in the Florida sun, how could I complain? Wally seemed happy staying in Florida for the winter… he's really a good guy … now that he's retired, it's foolish for him to stay home in the cold, gray winter, especially since I'm working. I'll commute every few weeks— I'm not ready to retire yet. Kids are all doing well, four beautiful and healthy grandchildren, a thriving counseling practice, good friends … I'm pretty lucky. I think airplanes are a good place to contemplate life. My tan looks pretty good, too. In spite of the cold weather, I'm looking forward to getting back to work … strange without Wally in the house. When I call to say good night, we laugh about my being a little nervous without him here … After forty-three years together, alone is not a condition I find myself in very often. Don't think about that now; think about planning stuff with friends …

February 27, 2002

… slept okay but that uneasy feeling has returned, and a strange image popped up during my morning meditation. I wonder what it means. The image is of a seemingly dead bush, pulled up out of the earth and suspended high above my head. It has one small, light

green root still alive. I wonder if it's about grieving my sister ... Is it telling me that I am no longer planted in the rich, firm soil of my family of origin? Although that would make the most sense, it doesn't feel right. Could it be about Wally? I am always concerned about his health with the diabetes and the smoking ... or, does it symbolize me—uprooted, suspended in air, clinging to life?

February 28, 2002

I am just ending a session with a client when the phone rings. It is my daughter-in-law telling me that Wally is in the hospital and that the doctors say he has a brain tumor. That's impossible! I was with him two days ago. He was tanned, relaxed, and looking forward to the beach. There must be a mistake.

I try to act like a rational human being. I go into my best crisis mode, cancel appointments and tell my waiting client that I cannot keep our appointment because my husband is in the hospital. When she asks what is wrong, I calmly say, "They think he has a brain tumor." She gasps, runs for the door, and never returns! Maybe I wasn't in my best crisis mode after all.

As I drive home, I think about our morning conversation. He did say he was going to check with the doctor because his mouth felt strange. His speech was fine. He said he looked and felt okay, so we didn't think too much of it. Of course, I immediately told him he should stop smoking, as usual! We laughed about the grandkids, talked about our plans for the rest of the day ... nothing out of the ordinary. I am sure this must be a mistake. You don't develop a brain tumor in two days!

As I think back on this time, I realize that our telephone conversation was the last carefree exchange we would have. For the next eight months, I lived in the presence of death, uprooted from the safety of the rich, firm soil of my life.

When tragedy strikes, there is no "right way" to manage it all; there is only "your way." You do the best you can. It is an emotionally confusing time. When we first hear of a life-threatening diagnosis, we are stunned. What we were doing just a minute before recedes into the background while our brain grapples with disbelief like a computer unable to decipher a configuration. Frantically, we grasp onto anything that suggests a hint of hope, scrambling to find the right treatment, the right doctor, the right hospital. Seeking to "fix it" refocuses our attention on providing some semblance of control while holding at bay an overwhelming sense of fear. As resources are exhausted without positive results, the meaning of this life-threatening diagnosis becomes clear, and fear firmly wraps its arms around your being. With this realization, the process of dying begins to unfold, joining the reality of everyday life along with cooking, cleaning and working. In the "blink of an eye," or so it seemed, I became a caregiver and an advocate for my dying husband.

As caregivers, many are able to rise above the fear and attend to the needs of their loved one. For others, the fear may be paralyzing—requiring assistance from friends, extended family members, hired help, and professionals in various fields. This does not mean you love the person in your care any less. As you see your loved one through this last period of life, the importance of self-care cannot be overstated. Often caregivers are so preoccupied, they forget to take in nourishing food, sleep when they can, or accept comfort from their friends. Attending to your needs helps you to better attend to your spouse's needs.

Helpful Hints for Survival

Moving through the initial stages of grief is all about basics. Find healthy ways to alleviate stress and keep stress low in other areas of life. Accept help when it is offered and ask for help when it is needed. Keep it simple.

* Shower daily and put on clean clothes
* Drink plenty of water—stay away from alcohol
* Make sure you eat nourishing food
* Go for a walk, get some fresh air
* Talk with friends daily
* Allow yourself to cry when the feeling arises
* Keep your hands busy; try knitting, drawing or puzzles
* Write about your feelings when you can. Sometimes you may be just too tired, but it is important that you speak what you feel, even if it is one word on paper.

Worksheet I

Reaction

When we first learn of our loved one's illness or death, we are so busy getting the help that's needed and notifying and calming others that very little consideration is given to ourselves. Therefore, the questions below offer a time to review what happened to you. Writing your thoughts and experiences will release the painful energy surrounding the memory of this time.

Where were you when you learned that your loved one was in danger or had died?

How did you react?

What was it like for you?

What images or dreams spoke to you that were helpful, insightful, or unsettling?

Chapter III
Our Life Together

Chrysalis of Sleep
Marcia Molay

Emotion will not rest.
I turn and toss till I spin
a quilted chrysalis of sleep,
wrap myself in its threads.

Gently twisting, blown by past breezes,
fine lines link dream and reality.
I draw those threads tighter until
restlessness forces consciousness.

I reach to touch you,
brush your toes, feel your heat.
Empty air—
… I remember.

Still disoriented,
no longer close to reality,
I glide above, lighting for a moment
to seek solace.

Crimson Bouquet

Helps the heart hold joyousness; for angelic
support when the heart is heavy; for sadness
from separation
—Delta Gardens

It was a cold, gray morning in October when Wally peacefully passed on. Later that day, as I sat numbly on my backyard swing, a hint of pink caught my eye from beneath the brown, fallen leaves. I pushed the leaves away to find a single, sweet pink flower snuggled in the dead leaves hovering against the cold. I smiled softly. I later identified the flower as a zinnia. The zinnia flower essence is helpful when there is too much somberness. It reminds us to smile.

I smile now, remembering how, at the tender age of eighteen, I plotted to get a date with the most popular boy in town. My girlfriends and I went to the movies every Sunday night. It was the meeting place for every teenager in town. Practically filling a middle row of orchestra seats, we surreptitiously watched the balcony for *him*. He was a college man and the best all-around athlete the city had ever seen. Everyone knew him. Every Sunday night, surrounded by his friends, he would squeeze his six-foot-five-inch, two-hundred-fifty-pound athletic body into a seat in the balcony. At least twice during the movie, he would sneak down to the lobby for a cigarette. However, he could not sneak past the eagle-eyed girls from the class of 1957. Once alerted, I would casually find my way to the water cooler where he always seemed to stand, leaning against the wall while mysteriously smoking a cigarette. I would extremely casually say, "Hi," and he would equally casually say, "Hi," back. This deep exchange went on all summer. My friend gave me a poem by Alice Hartick that captured the intensity of those meaningful greetings. Interestingly, the title is "Remembrance."

> You said so little I had to guess
> The thoughts that lay behind your steady eyes,
> But men who say a great deal more leave less
> To be remembered when their names arise.

Well, you can just imagine the stories I told myself! After I had consumed several gallons of water during that summer, our casual "Hi" became a conversation, and he started walking me home. Finally, my friends could relax and watch the movie instead of watching the balcony—our mission was accomplished!

I fell in love with his dark eyes and quiet ways on those walks home from the movies. As I came to know him, the mysterious athlete that I had a crush on from afar was replaced by a warm, gentle man who usually had a cigarette in his hand.

Back then, we thought smoking was sexy and sophisticated, and we all did it. We never thought to ask the question, "Is smoking dangerous to your health?" On those hot summer nights, as we took our first tentative steps toward building a life together, we thought sharing those cigarettes was so romantic—just like the movies. The memory is so clear, so innocent, and so happy … the movies on Sunday night.

Soon after our movie days, we planned our marriage. The year following his college graduation, we were married, and one month later, he left for California to play professional football. Just as the season began, he received a career-ending injury which brought him home. It was extremely disappointing for him. A childhood dream had been realized and then snatched away with a complicated twist of the knee. In his usual manner, he took the hit and moved on. He became a history teacher. He also coached track and field and football. We had our first child and joined the multitude of young couples trying to make ends meet, wondering if we would ever be able to afford the house in the suburbs.

During our child-focused years, we also had parents whose medical problems required our attention. We juggled our time between the children's activities and our parents' hospital stays.

We always took a little time for ourselves to reconnect. It was nothing spectacular—dinner, a movie, an occasional weekend without the children—but it was our way of ensuring that we still mattered to each other as a couple. Overall, our life was blessed with the ordinariness of daily living.

In order to buy that house in the "'burbs," Wally found a third job. After a day of teaching and coaching, he worked a part-time job to supplement our income. In between working, he attended graduate school. I was a stay-at-home mom monitoring the lives of three children and attending to the needs of our folks. Our plan was that when he finished graduate school, I could take that psychology course I was interested in. He was the one who urged me to take courses that led to a degree. For nine and a half years, that's what I did. I used to say, "Some people do garden club, I do school." In those days, it was phenomenal that a husband supported his wife getting a college education—at the so-called expense of the family. Just as he stood on the sidelines and cheered for our children to reach their dreams, he cheered for me. When I was offered a director's position that would make our tight schedule even tighter, he said, "Do it," and stepped in to help me.

As we became a seasoned married couple, we developed a nice, comfortable relationship without being possessive or demanding of each other. Although we enjoyed many of the same activities, there were some on which we could not agree. We liked the movies, but didn't always like the same type of movie. Our solution was to go to different movies that were playing close to the same time. He would go see his action movie with his candy bars and super-size Diet Coke, and I would go see my chick flick with my super-size popcorn (no butter) and water. Wally's passion was sports and history; mine was psychology and the arts. We found ways to blend these interests. I thought him to be particularly kind when he agreed to be backup if my opera partner cancelled. On one of our weekend getaways, we could not agree on where to eat. I wanted to go to a new Asian restaurant, but his favorite food was Italian. We agreed to go to the Asian restaurant for me where he would have coffee, then we would go to the Italian restaurant for him where I would have dessert. We had a grand time! When I started working, we planned my work schedule around his work schedule. He was home in the late afternoon to be with the children, and I could be at work without concern because my hours were in the late afternoon and evening. We shared cooking, cleaning, and child care. It was a relationship based on respect for each other's differences—even if we didn't like them—and an ability to compromise. We found that rhythm early in our marriage and kept it going until the end.

Wally was a quiet, unassuming man who knew how to listen. He had strength of presence I knew I could lean on. He was my anchor. I could turn to him whether it was about our children, my sick elderly parents, or my education. I don't want to idealize him, but in our forty-three years together, we just worked. We had our own stubborn qualities to be sure, but we could argue and not worry that we were not going to make up. We would banter back and forth matching wit and sarcasms with "attitude," the same way we saw our parents do with each other—that half-joke/half-truth that seemed to keep the relationship honest.

Our parents were very much a part of our life. One afternoon, we had to take my folks to a neighborhood clinic for some x-rays. Usually, one parent at a time worked best. This time, however, we were both called into action. I stayed with my mother while her doctor tried to tell her that her x-rays showed fluid around her heart. She told him the real problem was low potassium because her cousin had the same symptoms. While I tried to referee that discussion, Wally was with my eighty-seven-year-old father, who was having lung x-rays. As I came out of the doctor's office with my indignant mother, I saw my six-foot-five-inch husband holding my frail five-foot-four-inch father's arm and escorting him down the hall. My father, who was deaf, was causing quite a scene bellowing about how poor people could not afford health care. Wally, looking like a gentle giant next to my irate father, let him bellow until he was satisfied. Wally never complained about my parents' eccentricities. When he married me, he married my family. He always treated my parents as if they were his own. They loved him for it, and so did I.

Our later years became more difficult after we learned that Wally had diabetes. You see, Wally was a no-frills, meat-and-potatoes kind of guy. Change was not his style. Naturally, since I was eating homemade yogurt and he was eating double cheeseburgers and french fries followed by an ice cream shake, the topic of his diet, not to mention his smoking, became a bit of a focus. I would graphically describe how terrible his life could be if he didn't take care of himself, hoping that it would make him eat better and quit smoking. He would say he had never met a green bean he liked, then look nervous and light another cigarette. He could be so aggravating! I was either angry at his stubbornness or laughing at his craziness. Our children, grandchildren, friends, strangers, and doctors all tried as well, but to no avail. Somewhere during all of this, I thought if I divorced him, then that would make him stop. Then, I rationalized that he would only smoke more if I left, because we all knew he couldn't live without me. I decided that rather than be hysterical about the habit, I would respect his right to live his life as he chose. I understood the difficulty of addictions. He did decrease the amount of cigarettes he smoked, so I gave up being the health monitor, though I did continue to mention it on occasion.

Gradually, he became less enthusiastic about life. We still went out to dinner and the movies, but the socializing dropped off because it became tiring for him. We blamed the diabetes. He summoned his energy for an event, but afterward he was noticeably fatigued. I would kid him about becoming like his father, who went to bed at 7:30 every night. Slowing down bothered him. Wally was a former athlete and coach. He would make attempts to work out, smoke less, and eat better, but he couldn't seem to sustain them. Little did we know that the cancerous tumors were already growing in his body, slowly taking away his strength and his life.

Helpful Hints for Remembering

Some find remembering the relationship painful because it accentuates the sense of longing that permeates every day. For others, remembering is like a vacation from grief—for a little while, we can get lost in our memories of happier times.

Allow yourself some private time to be with your thoughts. Record those thoughts and memories either on paper or with a tape recorder. You may not be able to bring yourself to do this right away, but please, do it when the time is right for you. Your children and grandchildren will be happy to have your memories to look back on. Although the process may be sad in the beginning, it is also freeing. Remembering is an attempt to bring balance to your life. You can't ignore that you had a life with the person, regardless of the quality of that life. Remembering those earlier times lifts the weight of that sorrow. With each memory, we let go a little more and yet, remain close.

Helpful Hints for Remembering:

* Gather your pictures. Make a collage or select one picture to keep near you.

* Find a piece of jewelry or article of clothing that belonged to your loved one, and keep it with you.

* Make a ritual of visiting your place of worship, housed in a building or in nature, and have a conversation with yourself, your loved one, or your God.

* Mention his or her name in conversation with friends when it seems appropriate.

Worksheet II

Remembering

The relationship you had with your loved one was a special one. As with all special encounters, we want to honor our days together. Write a story about your life with your loved one. Some questions to consider are:

How did you meet?

What was he/she like?

What did you like about him/her?

What did he/she do that made you angry?

How did you make up?

Feelings of regret at this time are normal, believing life could have been different, if only ... Do you have any regrets?

Describe the best and the worst parts of the relationship.

Chapter IV
The Journey Begins

Out of the Depths

She went with him
to the place
of uncharted lands
where he wasted away
to a willow,
the ache of a branch
falling from her limbs,
crashing hard to
the ground
that once held her
sure footed and strong
The journey was
one she had
taken before,
but not as
a mother, daughter,
sister, lover,
partner or wife.

Out of the depths
she cries
with an ache,
that transcends
comprehensible dimension,
that reverberates loss
like an arrow
shot in the air,
like a mirror
suddenly
flash blinding
the human eye.

Out of the depths
she cries,
and cries,
until her
face furrowing tears
salt-preserve memories,
to be kept
in the hole
that now
shadows
her heart.

Onion

For releasing sadness;
Helps in all phases of grieving
—Delta Gardens

It took a while to understand what the doctor was telling me—and what he was not putting into words. *"Your husband has a brain tumor. We're not sure where it originates from ... We've given him medication to decrease the swelling ... If the swelling comes under control, we'll operate Monday ... We'll know tomorrow."*

In the fog of confusion that seemed to accompany his words, I asked, *"And what will happen if the swelling doesn't go down?"* As I asked the question, the answer became obvious. The frenzy of what to do now took over. Do I go to Florida to be with him or make arrangements for him to fly home tomorrow? Would that be an option?

Taking Protection Blend to help smooth the frenzied energy I felt throughout my body helped me to think rationally. I called friends for help and doctors for advice. When Wally and I were finally able to talk, it was difficult to find our voices in this ocean of fear. We cried our way through that telephone conversation, making plans to wait it out and come home to familiar surroundings. Fortunately, the swelling decreased, and after a little negotiation with the doctors, they allowed him to fly home. He walked off that plane looking tanned, relaxed, and smiling. The rest of my family looked like we needed a vacation. We went directly to the hospital and met with the brain surgeon.

We thought we had a window of possibility when the brain surgery was successful. His speech and balance were appropriate; we were very hopeful. When the results of the bone scan showed the cancer had spread to the femur bone, we found out he needed another operation so that he could walk. The diagnosis was lung cancer, which had metastasized to the brain and the bone. The prognosis was eight months to live without chemotherapy and maybe an additional three months with chemotherapy. The window of possibility shut tight.

After a short stay at a rehabilitation hospital, Wally returned home, walking with the aid of a walker and a cane. Within a short time, we fell into a routine that became normal for us. He organized all of the paperwork, cleared the drawers, and showed me what was needed and what was not. After radiation, hospice came in to help him with medicines and showers and all the other wonderful things that the nurses, aides, and volunteers do. While they were there, I went to work and felt normal for a little while. Friends would visit, and we would talk of old times and laugh. As he became weaker, the mood became more somber. I would wake up early, empty his urinal, go downstairs to the kitchen, prepare his insulin needle, make coffee, and bring it on a tray to the bedroom. We would sit quietly, waiting for his pain medicine to kick in, and then we would sip our coffee, discussing the night, the pain, and the daily expectation. It was calm, organized, and routine.

Wally was not a man of drama—and our family followed his lead. It's not that we are not emotional. It's just that we become pretty task oriented and very good at normalizing the effects of a trauma by creating a calm exterior. Simply put, we are a football family. My husband played professional ball until an injury stopped him; my two sons are retired professional football players. You see, in football, you learn to take the hit, shake it off, and move on. We did it while my daughter fought, and won, her battle with breast cancer. We did it while Wally fought, and lost, his battle with lung cancer. Privately, however, we were all very emotional and exhausted. The one glitch in this pattern is that I'm not really football material; I just married and raised football players. While my husband and kids were being stoic, I was spraying flower essences in all the rooms to raise the energy level. Angelica and Golden Amaranthus were my favorites. Angelica provides protection and guidance during life-changing experiences such as birth and death. Golden Amaranthus helps you move with the flow of life. I believe these flower essences eased our burden and cleared a small space for us to "let go and let God."

Time seems to disappear when you're involved in a crisis. One minute, we were laughing in the Florida sun; the next, Wally was struggling to climb a flight of stairs. His primary motivation was to not become bedridden. With the exception of one week, he came downstairs to the living room every day and climbed back upstairs every night, step by step. I held my breath as I worried he would fall. The excruciating pain Wally experienced would have stopped most in their tracks, but he never complained. It became a challenge for him. The memory is still painful.

One Saturday morning, he slipped in the shower and was too weak to lift himself out of the bathtub. I was no match for his large frame, and we were unable to contact our children. We realized we needed to use our heads not our muscles. We needed a strategic plan. I made coffee, and we settled back to think—he in the tub, me on the floor. We actually laughed at our dilemma and were proud of our ingenuity when we figured out how to get him out of the tub without further damage.

Wally was a brave man. Chemotherapy was the worst time for us. He kept up a good front but became more hopeless with every hair he lost. In the morning, as he showered, I would vacuum up the fallen hair that hid in that space between the end of the mattress and the headboard so that he didn't have to see how much had slipped from its roots as he slept. Our sons took him back and forth for treatment, often holding him up, because he was unable to walk on his own. When Wally played college football, his coach would say to him, "You're big enough to hunt bears." His students referred to him as the gentle giant. The chemotherapy treatment brought him to his knees. As it became obvious that the chemo was not effective, he decided to stop it. Then, we waited.

Waiting for a loved one to die is not the romantic portrayal we are accustomed to seeing in the movies. Watching Wally become increasingly weak, unable to breathe without oxygen, and unable to speak until the drugs kicked in to mute the pain did not strike me as particularly romantic. There was no beautiful background music, just the quiet droning of the television to momentarily distract us and fill the heavy silence. The knowledge that Wally might not be here tomorrow left me speechless. I had a hard time wrapping my mind around that thought. As difficult as times were, I could not pray for it to be over because then he would be gone. Yet, I could not pray for him to live because he would be in more pain. At one time when he seemed to be getting stronger, I told him that we might have more time than we thought. He whispered, "Please, don't wish that on me."

I don't think my husband ever showed fear, even when we talked about the afterlife. They were not long conversations, just passing thoughts that he would casually verbalize, as if it were the most natural of discussions. He said things like, "If I knew where I was going, maybe I wouldn't mind so much," or "Maybe I'll see Nan and Bob [my sister and brother-in-law] and we'll have a few laughs." He promised to let me know if he could. On one lovely summer afternoon as we were sitting on the porch, he asked where I was going to have the get-together. I was confused until the look on his face told me he was referring to his funeral. He did not seem fearful, just curious about where our family and friends would gather afterward.

Throughout his illness, friends and family came to visit. During the day, the house was filled with love and activity. However, the nights were lonely and long. In the quiet moments of the evening, after he fell asleep, unwanted thoughts about how things would play out would enter my mind. Although the essences provide a cushion against the pain, they also make room for expression. Over the months, it became easier for me to sleep in the room across from our bedroom. The doors faced each other, so I could lie on the bed watching him sleep. The intensity of Wally's illness would come crashing down on me, and I would sob quietly into my pillow. As I prayed for strength, the inner vision of a white snow lion running across snowcapped mountains would lull me to sleep.

People would say how wonderful it was to have the time to talk and say good-bye. I imagine I too might have felt that way if Wally died suddenly. I don't mean to imply that I am not grateful for our time together; it is just that I would trade all our conversations not to have had to watch his suffering. Although it is less painful to remember these conversations now, the memory of his ordeal is hard to value.

During this time, the therapeutic process of interactive imagery, accessed through the art of deep relaxation, helped me express my hidden or numbed feelings through the symbolic language of the imagination. Several of these journeys are included to help tell my story. The following brought me a sense of spiritual holding.

> **I arrived at an empty cave that was reddish brown in color with a solid floor and high cavern-like walls. In the center was a pool of water that disguised an opening to a deeper well. After I had examined the cave for a few moments, the forms of Kuan Yin, White Buffalo Woman, and the Blessed Virgin Mary appeared. They come to hold me, protect me. I am told to draw upon them for my sustenance and they will sustain me. There is no death here. A wave of fullness comes from within me, expanding and filling me.**

They also brought the wisdom of understanding the life cycle in a unique and gentle encounter. This journey about transformation helped me accept the natural flow of life.

I come to a small clearing where the sunlight is brighter. There are three trees. The one that I am drawn to is very tall, slender, and strong. It is a sturdy, stately elm, whose bark is flawless. It tells me that it is okay to have one's head in the sky if one's roots are deep into the earth. I like the image; it feels very healthy and wise.

Soon, I feel a sense of the second tree, which stands close by the tall, sturdy elm. This tree feels bigger, older; it is like the essence of the tree. I feel it to be softer, more transparent than solid; the bark is rougher, as if it has seen many years and storms. Its branches are lower and full. It is friendly and warm and loving, with a feeling of softness. It is the essence of the tree, the soul of the tree. It speaks to me of love and being linked with all things. She teaches me that when we die, we transform into something else. The plant kingdom, the animal kingdom, the human kingdom, and the heavenly kingdom are all connected. As we talked, I notice a third tree.

This third tree has no bark and no leaves. It is thin and frail but standing. It is dying. Soul tree tells me to wrap my arms around this dying tree. I make a circle with my arms and fill the circle with the golden light of love. The tree dissolves, and in its place comes one small green leaf. It is the lesson of transformation.

As the end drew near, Wally was unable to move out of bed, unable to hold a glass. He was easily distracted and confused. He ran a high fever all day, moving around in the bed as if he were trying to find a comfortable position. Although the symptoms were clearly connected to the brain tumor, I thought he may have had the flu. How the psyche protects one in the face of reality. Two days passed and by the time the fever had subsided, Wally had slipped into a peaceful sleep. I had been sleeping by his bed during this time. Sometime around 4:00 AM Saturday morning, I had what felt like a semiconscious dream.

I was pulled toward a spiral of light; I could see and feel myself moving. I felt my body float upward into a foggy place where I discovered my husband floating and looking lost. I took his hand, and we floated upward through the fog until we reached the crest of an opening. Reassuring him that he was safe, I left him standing at the crest of an opening waiting to move forward. I had accompanied him as far as I could.

I awoke not fully realizing what had happened, but knowing that his final breath would be soon. Throughout the day and evening, our family sat by his side silently praying and listening to him breathe. Sunday morning at eleven minutes past seven, his breathing stopped.

Death moved into our home on February 28, 2002, and left with my husband on October 20, 2002. During the "in-between" time, it waited in the corners of the rooms while cancer did its destructively cruel dance. It was frightening to be in its company, and I was angry at it. About six months after Wally died, the following journey helped me understand death in a different way.

I feel something dark and heavy hanging onto my leg. I cannot seem to shake it free. The more I struggle, the tighter it feels. "What is this?" It shows me a hidden figure that feels tired and sad. "Who are you?" I ask. I feel afraid and struggle even more. I say angrily, "What do you want here?" It speaks. "Illness invades the physical body, does whatever it wants, then makes living unbearable for everyone. Death comes to stop the suffering and return us to the Light."

I never truly understood why others would say, "Death is a blessing." It never felt like a blessing to me. For me, death was just another name for separation—and who wants to be separated from a loved one? In retrospect, I suppose I had to witness what true suffering was like—the kind of suffering that can't be stopped—before I could appreciate the "blessing" death brings. After this journey, it seemed so obvious.

The day-to-day process of living in the presence of death becomes surreal. As I said in my introduction, it was as if I were watching a movie in a strange theatre. The flower essences helped soften the harshness of the reality while keeping me in touch with what needed to be done. The journeys spoke to me in a manner that brought clarity to what I was experiencing. They helped me accept the life cycle transition and understand it as a new beginning. They gave voice to my inner strength at a time when I felt I had none. I encourage everyone to explore these two healing models.

Helpful Hints for Self-Nurturance

Caring for a loved one with a terminal illness leaves caretakers physically and emotionally exhausted. Taking care of yourself is vital. The essences were self-nurturing for me both during and after my husband's passing. The interaction with imagery during the journeys taps into the wisdom within you that helps you to heal. Therapy is a form of self-nurturance, not a sign of weakness. It helps you care for yourself. Whether it is in the form of inner journeys, flower essences, or traditional talk therapy, this is the time to include yourself in all that loving care that you pour into others. The goal of your self-nurturing is to prioritize your needs. This is not selfish. Whether you are alone or responsible for others, you need to stay emotionally and physically healthy.

* Always take care of the body first with rest, relaxation, healthy nutrition, and exercise.

* Do not neglect your physical well-being. The strain of your experience takes a physical toll on you. Keeping yourself healthy is vital.

* Find ways to organize the bits and pieces of your life.

* Your living arrangements have changed, whether you have moved or not. Assess each room of your home, and find what needs to be repaired, replaced, or given away.

* In between attending to your body and your living space, take those warm, soothing baths. Try a facial and a massage—and don't forget to give yourself words of encouragement.

* Reacquaint yourself with your spiritual practices.

* Find a bereavement therapist and/or join a bereavement support group with whom to share your thoughts.

Worksheet III

Consoling Ourselves

The memories we hold about the death of our loved one are often buried deep within us. We want to forget because it brings great sorrow when we think about them. However, in order to move forward, we need to let ourselves remember and, by remembering, release the painful energy surrounding those memories.

If there was time together before that special person died, write about the details of how you felt and what you did during those days and nights. If there was not time, write about that and what it was like for you.

What helped you: ritual, prayer, visiting familiar places …?

How do you console yourself for your loss?

Chapter V
Uncharted Territory

When you have come to the edge
of all the light you know
and are about to step out into the
darkness of the unknown
Faith is knowing that
one of two things will happen:
there will be something to stand on
... or ...
you will be taught to fly.
—Elizabeth Kübler-Ross

Borage
Gives peace, lightness, and courage; brings relief to burden, depression, and melancholy
—Delta Gardens

The dreaded day has come and gone. I waited numbly in my backyard as his body was taken from our home. Wally has died, and I'm still alive. I remembered my sister saying after her husband had died, "I'm just biding time." Now, I know exactly what she meant. My life had ended. I could not imagine a tomorrow without him.

During the wake, before the mourners arrived, while looking at all the beautiful flowers people had sent, I surreptitiously sprayed Rescue Remedy, the flower essence known to bring calmness to high-stress situations. And I really needed that Rescue Remedy when one woman offered her condolences by saying "Just wait, it gets worse." I'm sure her intention was not to forewarn of doom and gloom, but I would not recommend this form of support, especially at a wake.

I am not a big fan of funerals, but as funerals go, I think we all did pretty well. Many loving, caring people attended, which was very comforting. My son gave an eloquent eulogy and my grandson told a funny, endearing story about his Papa. Funerals are such private affairs, I think it's enough to say that unlike my Italian relatives of yesteryear who would, literally, throw themselves on the grave, we did not wail or cause a scene

As the formality of dying ended and I attempted to bring some normalcy to my daily existence, I found myself asking unanswerable questions—the "why" questions. For me, it wasn't, "Why did he die?" I knew why: Cigarettes are dangerous to your health. He was a smoker; that's the risk you take. For me, the questions went more like, "Why him and not the person who wreaks havoc on the lives of others? Why not the murderer? Why not those awful people who hurt children?" They were useless thoughts that served no purpose, other than to rub salt into the open wound. But that little voice inside, the voice that reasons like a child, would think, "I bet those people smoked …" Maybe they did, but it wasn't their time. I believe it was just Wally's time— whether he smoked or not. Along with the "why" questions came the "God" questions. How does God decide who lives and why? Does God have a plan? Questions about the meaning and purpose of life—questions about whether or not there is a meaning or purpose to life—followed. These questions are better explored with one's spiritual advisor. This is not the time to make sense of it all.

Once that internal philosophical discussion quieted down, the next looming questions were, "How do you go on living in a world so changed? What inspires you to get up in the morning and move through your days?" For the young widow with children, I can imagine that the children can become the inspiration for living, even though I know that for some, the pain of loss is so great that even this most important reason doesn't suffice. But for those whose children are grown or those who have no responsibilities for others, how do we find that inspiration? And more immediately, "How do I transform the painful memories that filled my home?"

I immediately found myself trying to remove all signs of the illness that pervaded our house. I started in our bedroom, throwing out just about anything that wasn't nailed down. The chair he sat in, the bedcovers, trays that held medicines, glasses, pictures on the walls, clothes I wore during the funeral, all were donated or dumped in a desperate effort to erase painful memories. I knew I had to sleep in our bedroom, the room Wally had died in, or I might never have the courage to enter it again. When it was time for bed, I held my breath as I entered the bare, cold room, pulled the covers over my head, and mercifully fell asleep.

All the rooms in the house were in disarray, filled with the beautiful flowers people had sent. In order to find a place to sit, my children, my niece, and I had to clear the rooms. While we were at it, I had them rearrange the furniture. This started a redecorating frenzy. I painted walls, changing things around as much as the structure of the rooms would allow, adding and replacing "stuff" in every area of the house. The bedroom I had feared entering became my safe haven. I climbed in bed as early as I could, grateful to have made it through the day. I would snuggle under the covers and watch the Home and Garden channel—sometimes all night. I went to bed so early that I was never tired. I didn't read because I could not concentrate, so I took up knitting. I never made anything, just knitted one and purled two. I've come to know this as excellent therapy. It kept my mind focused and my hands busy. This went on for months until I realized that I was thinking of buying a chair for the bedroom in order to be more comfortable. That's when I reminded myself that there were other rooms to live in.

At night, I had strange dreams, some I understood and others I just accepted.

One of my dreams found me standing in my foyer trying to turn on the lights. The lightbulb in the floor lamp was missing. I tried the ceiling lights as I called upstairs to Wally that the lights were not working … no answer … I called downstairs saying the same thing, thinking the power must have gone out. There was no answer. I was wondering where he was when suddenly he appeared on the staircase. I noticed he looked pale but I didn't say anything about it. I said, "The lights won't work."

He sat down at a desk and started to look at some bills and paperwork. He then got up from the desk and lightly pressed his head against the wall. I knew he was upset with himself but then he was okay. He moved into the kitchen and was midway down the staircase leading to the fuse box as he told me something about the circuit box not being big enough to hold everything and that was why it was dark … He looked up and asked me what I wanted turned on. I was puzzled that he should ask that question and said, "I want everything turned on." He gave me a sweet smile filled with love and approval. I smiled back and noticed again how pale he was ... like when he was sick. As he started to go downstairs, I realized that everything was brightly lit.

I woke up screaming and crying and was frightened for what felt like a long time. I called a friend. The time was 4:30 AM.

There was no disguising the deep sense of emptiness that pervaded every moment. I'm a pretty self-sufficient person, but learning to live independently is quite challenging when you have operated as part of a couple. Coming home to an empty house made me cringe, especially after dark. Making decisions was confusing. Home maintenance issues created unnecessary worry. My anxiety about home repairs was not a big deal in and of itself, but collectively with other feelings of uncertainty, I found myself being unnecessarily reactive about situations. Freud once said that all behavior is purposive. In addition, the famous "they" say, "Ya gotta do what ya gotta do." With those two authorities in mind, I reconstructed my behaviors to help me cope with my emotions. I rearranged my schedule, asked others for advice about the simplest of things, and became very cautious about drinking that relaxing glass of wine. As a former substance abuse counselor, I knew the timing was dangerous. Grief has a way of lulling you into a disconnected state and alcohol can only make it worse.

Experiencing a traumatic event heightens our sensitivities to anything that remotely resembles pain or trouble. Our sympathetic nervous system is working overtime like a guard dog pacing the boundary of our property ready to pounce at the least sign of intrusion. It takes time to adjust and to build self-confidence about carrying out responsibilities that fell in the other person's domain. Flower essences lend themselves nicely to these unexpected times. A personalized blend from a practitioner or a trip to a health store for Bach's Mimulus can help decrease known fears and restore balance.

The physical body also reverberates with the pain of grief. The stress of the vigil often weakens the immune system, and we become susceptible to illnesses. Mind/Body medicine teaches us to listen to our body. It sends messages in the form of aches, pains, colds, and headaches, which keep us from doing things— things we don't know we are not ready to do. I call these messages *resistances.* I chose to listen to my resistances instead of forcing myself to break through them.

Many years ago, I counseled a young boy whose mother had died. He could not leave his house to go to school or to the playground near his home. As his therapist, I was naturally concerned about his slipping into a depression. Now, I know and feel the depth of that resistance he experienced. It's as if a switch is thrown and you can't move. I've planned trips with friends, but when the time came to make the reservations, I couldn't go through with it. It felt as if someone had tied a sash around my midriff and harnessed me to my house. As with my client, who resumed his school attendance, after a while, I began to do things again.

As the trauma slowly subsided, I became aware of "feeling" again. I had been numb and now, I was thawing out. My sensations seemed to be heightened. I could feel the emptiness of the space he once filled. I could feel the air of that space on my skin. The sorrow was profound, deep, and wrenching. As my mind tried to make sense of what was happening, I felt my heart hurting as if there was a hole there that I was unable to seal. It seemed to fill with sorrow, empty through tears, and then fill again; it was never ending.

During the journeying experience, it is customary to engage in conversation with the images that appear and ask what they have come to tell us. I asked the hole in my heart what it had to tell me, and it answered:

I am the vastness out of which you come. I am the non-connection to the physical world which you live in. There is no separation from Source here. There is only Light. This hole in your heart

is the portal through which the Light flows to heal you and others like you. It is not aloneness you feel; it is the vastness of the universe where all things flow from and return to. It stretches your heart to open to the Light. This is what is called the Spiritual Connection. It is with you and others always. Some feel it through their religion and call it many names. Others feel it through nature. For you, my dear, it is receiving the Spirit in its non-physical state.

And so it went. I was thoroughly focused on one day at a time, learning as it unfolded. It was odd being unable to think about tomorrow or remember yesterday. The nights were long, and each day passed without connection to the day before or the day to come. I felt like a character in the movie *Groundhog Day* where each day repeated itself over and over. Eventually, the days started to weave together and then there were weeks. The nights took longer. It was after 10:00 PM that the hours were the most hollow, the time when you are truly alone with yourself and your memories. I filled those hours with writing and television.

A "good night's sleep" was the hardest to accomplish, but the flower essences again came to my aid in the form of the Morning Glory essence which helped bring rhythm to my sleep. The balancing quality of the essences is found in the signature of the plants—its own specific energetic purpose. The petals of the morning glory flower open in the morning and close at night. It helps calm the nervous system, which can enhance one's ability to sleep. We know that stress creates an imbalance in body functioning, commonly showing up in digestive and sleep issues. Morning Glory and other flower essences help rebalance the system. Taking the essence or essences daily or as needed is a decision made according to need. It took a while but eventually, my body got it, and my sleep became regulated just like the flower's petals opening in the morning and closing at night.

Finding my way through the early days of recovery, struggling with the depth of sadness and starkness of aloneness, I started to wonder how long it would last. It seems interminable but it does change. That's the uniqueness of this experience of grief. It is different for everyone, and everyone moves at his or her own pace. The most common feeling described by others and experienced by me is a feeling of disconnection, particularly during the first twenty-four months. From the moment Wally died, I struggled to reconnect with my life.

In the beginning, I found myself "going through the motions," doing things the same way as before. There is a false sense of security attached to keeping things as they were, but it is short-lived. Soon the realization comes that things have to change. For instance, a simple thing like food shopping becomes a major decision event—to buy or not to buy? I questioned almost every decision I made. Once I accepted that change needed to happen, I made small adjustments —like drinking tea instead of coffee, making myself eat dinner at the table instead of in front of the television.

Clients have asked me, "How did you know what to do?" I can only reply, "I didn't know." I remembered what I had counseled others to do—strive for balance. Gradually, an internal knowing floated into my conscious awareness that things need to shift, even though it was never quite clear about what needed to shift. What I did know was that I needed to do something. I asked myself what I was interested in; the answer came back, "Nothing." Then I asked, if I were happy, what I would be interested in. That yielded an answer which led me to take classes in anything that was different from what I knew. Did I enjoy them? Not really. But, I went anyway. When I signed up for the art class, I thought I would learn to draw flower vases. Instead, it turned out to be an advanced class drawing male and female nude models. Oh well.

I started noticing how I felt physically, as well as emotionally, and took steps to improve on that. I meditated more and prayed a lot. I stopped giving myself a hard time about how I felt and why. Whenever I was self-critical, I pictured my loved ones reassuring me. When I thought about something negative, I changed it to something positive. I became my internal cheerleader—not an easy feat, I might add, when you feel life has left you in the lurch. But if I didn't give myself words of encouragement, who would—especially when to the outside world, I looked like I was doing "just fine."

From a therapeutic perspective, I would say that I applied the concepts of cognitive-behavioral therapy and mind/body medicine to myself. Simply stated: what you think, you feel and do; changing your thinking will change how you feel and how you behave. Eventually, new routines emerged that gradually turned into a new foundation. What seemed impossible starts to happen. The individual days connected, the long nights got shorter, my disrupted sleep improved, and somehow I noticed I felt a little better. Hope seeped into my awareness.

It's a strange thing this sense of hope. My trusty dictionary defines hope as "the feeling that what is desired is also possible" In the beginning, I hoped for his recovery. When it was clear that it was not going to happen, hope died for me. Living without hope is like living without fresh air to breathe. So, feeling a sliver of hope that maybe, just maybe, these vacuous days and nights were beginning to resemble what I remembered as "normal" brought a great sense of relief. The famed mind/body teacher, Herbert Benson, MD, refers to this state as *remembered wellness*. It became a motivator urging me on to find ways to help myself. I did the usual friends and family lunches and dinners but with much more enthusiasm for the encounters. I signed up for courses, attended lectures, plays, musical events, and only went to light, airy movies—no deep, intense movies for me! I forced myself to think with more optimism.

One of the starkest realities I encountered when Wally died, regardless of good friends and a loving family, was that I am responsible for taking care of myself. It is me who brings me a nice cup of tea when I have a cold. It is me who reminds me to take it easy when I've been working too long. It is me who cheers me up when I am down. In the past, Wally shared in all those thoughtful, nurturing behaviors. Now it is important to know what I want and need and when I should have it. In so doing, I reconnected with the deepest part of myself, reigniting and nurturing a sense of hope that "what I desire is also possible."

Helpful Hints for Reconnection

This is a time of reconnecting with yourself and your living space. Start exploring new hobbies and different interests. Try on new behaviors. At first, you may have to coax yourself into trying something new, then one thing leads to another and you build increased willingness to seek what's right for you.

Helpful hints for bringing you back to you:

* Establishing a routine of behavior is helpful during the early stages of living without your loved one. Simple and predictable are the guidelines to follow. Try a daily walk at the same time each day or lunching with someone twice a week.

* Make a daily to-do list and do at least two things on the list, or more if you can.

* Remember your dreams, and write them down. They may be a source of inspiration or clarification.

* Start noticing where you hold tension in your body. When you notice an ache or pain, allow yourself to stop, take three deep breaths focusing on the area of discomfort, and ask yourself what caused this to happen. Your body is sending a message for you to decipher. Listen to your inner voice.

* Be really kind to yourself—as if you were your friend.

* Make healthy choices, not just with your diet but with your actions. Opt for exercise instead of being a couch potato. Identify one positive thing, seen or done, each day.

* Surround yourself with color and beauty.

* Write yourself a letter each week (or day) identifying the courageous things you did to keep your spirit up, and congratulate yourself for making it through.

Worksheet IV

Finding Our Way

Reestablishing our life while grieving often involves experiencing feelings that are unfamiliar and behaviors that may be out of the norm for us. The goal of these survival tactics is to fill the time, heal the wound, and ease the pain. Some of the things that we do we might consider silly; some of our choices we might frown upon and feel guilty about. As we reconnect with our creative side and/or our rebellious side, we can learn tolerance, patience, and forgiveness for ourselves—a reconnection with self that is nurturing and not judgmental.

What feelings and behaviors seemed to dominate your time of heightened emotional pain?

How did you navigate through those early days of grieving?

What messages were sent as guidance through your dreams?

What did you learn about yourself that you didn't know before?

Chapter VI
Pack Up Your Sorrows

New Relationship
Marcia Molay

I brought my coffee today
sit on the stone wall
talk to you.

We can't keep meeting like this.
Time to redefine our relationship
this sad separation.

Conflicted concerns—
unable to accept the void
unable to reject it
I still need to test ideas
toss them to you
float them in still air.

Unlike your camera lens
I am fixed focus
focused on now.
My far-sighted eyes
can't see right in front of me
without your prism
your down-to-earth sense.

A homely image,
a paradigm of place
to bring us
not to peace
not to acceptance
but to rest.

Sumac
*Assists in maintaining connection with the heart
during difficult phases and transitions in recovery,
brings stamina to the individual*
—**Delta Gardens**

It was our home for thirty-six years—the place where we raised
our kids, argued, and loved, the place where he died. Now, our
home felt empty and oppressive. The following journey captured
my innermost feelings.

> **I am walking down a path in the woods when
> I come to a clearing where there is a wise man
> sitting on a large boulder-like rock. He points
> to the side where a narrow river flows but its
> course is obstructed by a collapsed beaver dam.
> He tells me to look inside. I pick through the
> leaves, branches, and mud to find a beaver stuck
> in the debris. I pull him to the bank of the river
> where he lays barely breathing. I am uncertain
> whether he will recover or die.**

Like the beaver, I felt buried under my collapsed life. In an
attempt to rebuild, I shopped. Purchasing has always been a favorite
pastime of mine, and I would like to take a moment to pay homage
to the art of retail therapy (within one's budget, of course). I love
buying clothes, pulling an outfit together, and finding a bargain.
However, I couldn't do any of that. I had lost the sense of who I was.
Consequently, no style was appealing and no bargain enticing—a
side effect of grief, I thought. Although my "fashion sense" had
been compromised, the nesting drive was active.

I found the greatest relief in shopping centers and home goods
stores, of all places. It was the easiest resource to access. While I have

friends who cringe at the thought of going to a shopping center, it was the perfect distraction for me. I could blend into the crowd, pretending to be involved in a normal everyday activity. Plus, shoppers are so absorbed in their own missions, I never had to talk to or smile at anyone. And I found pleasant things to buy for my house.

To the average observer, it was redecorating; to me, I was balancing my emotions. The sadder I felt, the more I immersed myself in decorating. There was a lot to do. Everything broke, everything was expensive to fix, and everything took so long to complete. Even the soapstone sink in the basement that had been there since the house was built in 1920 cracked and had to be replaced. We had very old, tall pine trees growing in our backyard. During storms, they would sway back and forth so forcefully we would hope they wouldn't fall on the house. Sure enough, two months after Wally died, the large limb of one of the trees, hollowed out by disease, split off during a Christmas snowstorm. It landed in our driveway, just missing our house. The symbolism was profound. As the tree was cut down and removed, I remember crying, wondering who was directing this movie.

As I ran out of projects to focus on, I came to understand that there are three truths to the reality of loss:

* You understand the truth, even though it does not quite seem possible.

* You know it's true, even if you forget when you are out of the house.

* You come home to an empty house and are struck by the fact that it has really happened.

When I started to explore the idea of living somewhere else, I was surprised to find that I could not move away from my neighborhood. I felt it was all that I had left. It was a ridiculous feeling since I have a loving family and lots of friends. Nonetheless, the familiarity of the neighborhood provided a feeling of warmth and predictability—I knew the area. Without sounding too dramatic, the neighborhood held the last physical connection to the man I had lived with since I was twenty-one.

Fortunately, around the corner from my home, townhouses were being built. From my first meeting with the realtor to the last, I was always in tears. He really earned his commission! Within a month, my house had been sold, I had bought a new townhouse, and I was clearing out my "stuff."

Going through our belongings was difficult for all of us, but particularly for my children. They had to sort through all the mementos that we had collected over the years, reawakening memories of happier times, which now were bittersweet.

As I sat in my kitchen for the last time, I felt as if I were going through the funeral for the first time. I had been numb then, and from the way I felt as I closed the house, I think that was a gift. Even the weather played its part. It was a snowy morning in October when we buried my husband of forty-three years. It was a snowy morning in March when I closed the door to our home of thirty-six years. *Wrenching* is the only word that can adequately describe this state of emotion. A year had passed, but in my body and mind, it felt as if he had just died.

Once the details of selling and buying were finished, I felt a weight had been lifted from my shoulders. My new house held the promise of being easier to manage and the gift of no reminders. I was the first homeowner in the small townhouse complex. The buildings were beautifully finished, but empty. It resembled a movie set waiting for the cast to appear. As I stared out the window at this lifeless scene, I remembered the vision of the uprooted bush that had visited over a year ago. At that time, I wondered what this symbolic message was telling me. There was no doubt now. I was, clearly, uprooted from the firm, rich soil of my life, suspended in air, with one small green root, waiting for the cast and the spring to bring the stirrings of life.

When the decision to move is made there is a need for preparation, a gestation, if you will, of thinking and planning and imagining before actually moving that can help ease the pain of transition. Moving carries with it many unknowns, so the more open you are to change, the easier it is to adjust to your new surroundings. Always weigh and measure the pluses and minuses of what you are giving up and what you are gaining. Once you evaluate your situation and consult with trusted family and friends, you will know with little doubt what the best thing is for you to do.

Moving from the "old homestead" was sad and scary. At first, it was an unthinkable thought, then it became a possibility, and then it made perfect sense. For me, making the transition worked on many levels. As wrenching as it was, I feel it became the conduit through which the energy of life flowed back into me. Although moving is not necessary for healing, for me it was like breathing fresh air. Shortly after moving, I experienced a powerful journey that symbolized healing for me.

> **I am walking through a fog that seems to be the inside of a cloud. On a faraway cloud, I notice a flat figure that I know to be me, but it is just my skin, a deflated me. I am led by angels to the source of the Light that surrounds them. There are no words spoken here, but I know I am being healed. My body feels raw, as if there is no skin covering it. The Light starts to lay itself on my arms, legs, and whole body. It is a thin layer that covers the flesh and starts to heal me. I feel the hurt stopping as many more layers are added. I understand that another skin is waiting for me. It looks just like me. It is placed over me—over the Light that heals me. I am told that the trauma depleted me—the trauma of walking with death and bringing Wally to the threshold.**

I wasn't living in the balcony anymore.

Helpful Hints for Change

Change can be resisted or embraced. The choice is yours. If we learn nothing else from surviving our loss, we learn that choice is the dominating factor in recovery. We are responsible for our well-being. Your experience is unique to you; therefore, no one really knows the depth of distress you are in. It's not because others haven't experienced similar feelings or because people are not empathetic, it's because each person grieves in his or her own way. What may be awful for you may not be as bad for someone else. In addition, each person's coping skills are different. Joining a bereavement group where members can share their skills and insights benefits everyone.

* If change is difficult for you, do it in small increments. For example, change the placement of a chair, get rid of one corner of the clutter, or give away one piece of his/her clothing.

* If you can, delay making major life-shifting decisions during the first year. Things become clearer after a year of adjustment.

* For those who need to make important decisions during that first year, gather a group of trusted family or friends to brainstorm the idea with you before acting on it.

* Do something a little different when you can. It can be as simple as taking a new route home or as courageous as going to the movies alone.

* Try a different hairstyle—but you may want to rethink those pretty red streaks.

* If you decide to move to a new home or state or country, employ the art of pretending, turning the move into an exciting adventure.

* This is the time to tap into your imagination and ask, "If I were happy, how would I feel and act about this change?"

* Always ask, "Is this change in my best interest?"

Worksheet V

Changes

How do you embrace change?

What changes did you make after the funeral?

What was it like for you then?

How did you decide the time for change was right for you?

List three changes you are ready to make right now.

List three changes you can plan to make in the next year.

Chapter VII
From the Balcony to Center Stage

When we allow it, grief leads us on a path of self-discovery.

—CLB

Lovage
For those who want to make changes in their lives
—Delta Gardens

Time to move on, "they" say ... but ... to where? The natural flow of daily living was about all I could manage in those early days and months. I considered it an accomplishment if I slept through the night. Even though I knew I was processing my pain during sleep, it was still annoying to watch paid-advertising promotions in the middle of the night. Entering my house without dread, remembering to eat healthy food, trying to read the newspaper—things I took for granted before—were now all accomplishments, behavioral measurements of recovery I would have identified had I been at work. I really never thought grief would be so tedious.

I finally got it that Wally was not returning when an acquaintance asked, "Have you dated yet?" I gave some bumbling answer in an attempt to cover up my shock because the idea was so foreign to me. It wasn't foreign to my husband, though. One day, as I was cooking dinner, he mentioned casually, "You know you can get married again." I was so surprised I gruffly shook my head no and passed it off as a silly thing to think about. Then, to lighten the heaviness of the mood, I dramatically said, "But wait a minute, if he's a millionaire and dances very well, we might talk."

Therapeutically, a new relationship may be exciting, but it is not a necessary component of moving on. However, feelings about dating are important to consider because it helps to wade through the often unthinkable feelings of being with another. The real question is, "What does moving on mean and how do you know when it has taken place?" Does it mean finding another partner to live with the rest of your days? Does it mean finding something outside you, or does it mean to search for it within yourself? Or, is it all of the above?

A simple question for you, perhaps, but not for me. It is a question with a variety of answers and many different expressions demonstrated by the individual's personality and preferences. I have friends who are widowed who wouldn't miss a Friday night at the ballroom or the opportunity to spend time with a considerate companion/lover. Yet, in the basement of their homes, their deceased husband's belongings and other treasures from their former life remain intact. Then, there are others who have moved from their family home, have new surroundings, and have never even considered dancing with someone else. Through the years, I have counseled many men and women who entered into new relationships shortly after their loved one died. Some found happiness in their new relationship. Others slid into the depths of despair, reliving their partner's passing when that new relationship dissolved. Dating may be a sign of moving on, or it may be an attempt to avoid the pain of grief. The whole "moving on" thing is complicated. Behaviorally, you may look like you're doing it, but in my experience, it is how you feel that answers the question.

J. William Worden, a leading expert in the field of bereavement, writes about the Four Tasks of Mourning:

1.   Accepting the reality of the loss

2.   Working through the pain of grief

3.   Adjusting to an environment in which the deceased is missing

4.   Emotionally relocating the deceased and moving on with life

My experience with these tasks is that they repeat themselves continually until the strength of the sorrow diminishes. There is no timetable. I also recognize that there is no way out of this except through it. Just when I thought I had it under control, another pocket of sorrow bubbles up to the surface. Each time the release—the disbelief, the crying, the down feeling, the missing— is shorter until the memories become bittersweet and bearable.

I remember the first time I felt the feeling of being "happy" for no reason. It was on Sunday morning, Valentine's Day 2005. While making coffee, I heard myself humming. It had been a long time since I had heard this sound. I stopped to listen, and sure enough, it was me, humming. There, in the deep recesses of my heart, I felt a tiny stirring of joy. It felt remarkable. I had forgotten the sense of happiness. This feeling was not attached to any particular event; it was simply the feeling of being happy. I treasure this feeling and nurture it as much as I am able. I celebrated my discovery by playing a CD I had just purchased. As synchronicity would have it, the first words that shouted from the CD player were "Move on!"

I liken "moving on" to reconstructive surgery. You hold back from the surgery until one day, you can't move due to the excruciating pain, then you know it's time. Eventually, I realized that if I did not move out of the emotional pit that engulfed me, I could die there—and at times, that seemed like the most logical thing to do. However, reconstructing one's life goes rather slowly. "I just want to get back to normal," we say to ourselves, but what we thought of as normal is no longer. Noted authority on grieving, Kenneth Doka, PhD, states *"Transformative grief means that whenever we experience a loss, it changes us. And significant losses change us significantly."*

Everything I knew, I knew as a couple. Now, I was single. Some activities and habits that I clung to did not bring the satisfaction they once did. Some continued, but there is a lot of adjusting— adjusting to not having him around to talk to, or yell at, or make love with, or go on vacation with, or just to take out the trash. At first, my encounter with loss was all about my lost love. However, as my experience unfolded, I discovered that this journey through grief became a journey of self-discovery. In order to move on, we have to explore where and what to move on to—that entails experimentation.

I did a lot of seeking out, feeling my way through, and trying new things. Sometimes I wondered if it was all worth it, but then I realized that if I stopped exploring, I would become stagnant. And stagnation leads right back into the depth of grief. Please, do not mistake my activity as avoidance, although it often adds a nice distraction. The deeper purpose of my activity was to discover what I liked or disliked. It is how I found the inspiration to continue growing and developing my own interests. It helped me create a new way of living. So far, I have taken art lessons, an interior decorating course, gardening for flower boxes (I have a deck now), singing and tap-dancing lessons, and attended multiple lectures on a variety of topics. I figure that at the very least, in addition to singing and tapping my way through life, I will make (sort of) beautiful pictures of the flower boxes that decorate my deck, while contemplating the wisdom of yet another lecture.

Little by little, I emerged—two, three, five years later, a different person. Along the way, I got to know parts of myself for which I never had time. I came to know what I liked and wanted, rather than just making do with what I needed. I have a new respect for my ability to take care of myself and increased thoughtfulness about my emotional and physical well-being. I learned to rely on my own opinion, treating myself with compassion if I made a mistake. I indulged myself with kindness, as the good mother indulges her ill child, until the empty space around me and within me filled with a sense of comfortableness and security. Moving through loss brought me to the core of who I am. From there, I built my new life from the inside out.

I have come to understand that moving on is not just about changing one's address, dating, or even remarrying; it is not about forgetting. Moving on is about making a conscious decision to live—physically, emotionally, and spiritually. In no way does it imply that I was not afraid, that I knew where I was going, or that I knew what I was going to do. That's the adventurous side to moving on. Deciding to live means that deep inside, I let go of the hand that I held for many years and stood on my own—becoming a participant in the present. And by living in the present, I honor Wally's life and the life we lived together.

My profession is all about "knowing yourself." My emotional journey from the balcony to center stage taught me about myself in a way that no schooling could have. I have gained a much deeper understanding about feelings and behaviors and have learned a lot about trust—trust in myself and my ability to reach for health and healing. At some point during the "in-between" time, I asked Wally if he had any regrets. He thoughtfully answered, "I wouldn't have worried so much." More than ever, I want to make every day count. Wally would say to me, "As long as you're happy." My plan is to be just that!

On February 27, 2002, when that disturbing vision of the uprooted bush appeared just after that long-ago Florida vacation, I had no inkling of what was to come. When I had the following journey, I knew I was on the road to recovery.

> **Bear appears and invites me to walk deeper into the woods. The density of the tall trees does not let a lot of sunlight in but further up, I can see a shaft of light. We walk in the direction of the light and come upon a bush planted in the rich, fertile soil of this deep forest. Bear draws my attention to the tiny buds waiting to open.**

Helpful Hints for Self-Discovery

This is your final, yet never-ending, stage of recovery. You are out of the dark days of grief and into a more sunlit existence. You have set up a fresh living situation that you enjoy. You have learned how to entertain yourself. You have begun to sort out what you like to do and with whom. This is a time to strengthen the foundation you have built for yourself, both internally and externally. It may feel tentative at times, but with attention and commitment to your growth and development, your new foundation will become stronger—like you.

* Find at least one thing in your day that you think is positive.

* Each day, spend a little time with yourself and your spiritual guidance giving thanks and asking for what you want.

* Be aware of what causes you distress and get to the bottom of it as soon as possible.

* Take courses that stimulate your mind.

* Write in a journal or write your own story.

* If your schedule allows, volunteer somewhere.

* Remember, grief is something you *move through*, not get over. Let yourself ask for help when needed, and cry if the feeling arises.

* Have *fun*. Remember, your well-being depends on you.

Worksheet VI

Discovering

Write about three things you have learned about yourself through your journey of healing.

Do you think, feel, or act differently than you did before?

What are some interests you would like to pursue?

Introduce yourself to you.

Chapter VIII
Signals from the Beyond

I feel the energy of your love
surround me,
fill me,
reassure me
—I am not alone

—CLB

Bushy Violet Aster
For letting go of attachment to fear
—**Delta Gardens**

Many movies and television programs today have as their theme communication with dead people. There are mediums that will contact your deceased loved one. There are books about the afterlife and near-death experiences telling extraordinary stories about lights and tunnels. So what I am about to tell you should not be shocking. In fact, I bet you have your own paranormal experiences that you do not share with anyone, because you are afraid someone will think you've lost it.

When someone close to you dies, you naturally want to maintain some kind of connection with that person. We pray for them, talk with them, and some have even set plates at the dinner table for them. How often have you heard someone say, "I know my mother/my husband is watching over me"? J. William Worden's fourth task of grieving describes, "Emotionally relocating the deceased by gathering special memories thereby creating a new relationship with the lost love." You decide what is meaningful for you and how your new relationship with your loved one takes shape.

I attended a bereavement group where several women hesitantly spoke of odd occurrences after their spouses had died. Commonly reported was the feeling of their husband's presence in their homes. One widow commented that she felt a pressure on the side of the bed, as if her husband were sitting there. Others knowingly nodded their heads. One by one, you could see the sense of relief on their faces as they listened to each other's stories. "How long does this last?" asked a widow of five months as she reported that she hears her husband calling her name every morning. These experiences are a normal and acceptable part of grieving. I think of them as the alchemical way of adjusting to our loss—transforming distance into closeness.

When Wally and I talked about the afterlife, I asked him to

signal me if there was a way—a sort of "call me when you get there" kind of thing. Well, about three months after he died, his image flashed like a snapshot while I was meditating. He was sitting at an outside café, smoking a cigarette (some things never change). He seemed to be in conversation with two people whom I could not see but knew to be my brother-in-law and sister—just as he mentioned before he died. I can dismiss this experience as a projection from my unconscious, but I can't dismiss the following experiences.

Two and a half years later, a police officer stopped me for speeding. In my defense, I was not going very fast and there was very little traffic. As he was waiting for me to find my identification, I said, "Does it matter that I'm a widow?" hoping he would go easy on me.

He, of course, said, "No," as he took my registration and license back to his patrol car to write up the dreaded ticket. When he returned, he asked how long ago my husband had died. When I told him it was about two and half years ago, he appeared surprised then said, "Well, he must be looking after you because when I put your license into the computer, his picture came up." With that, the officer handed me a warning. I had purchased the car about a year previously, and it was registered in my name only.

On another occasion, about three years after Wally died, I found a diabetes test strip on my dining room floor during a family gathering. I noticed it as I was starting to serve dessert. It hadn't been there during the main course. Plus, nothing related to diabetes came with me to my new house. I cannot logically explain how a diabetes test strip found its way to my dining room.

I include this short discourse of my experience because it was a part of my journey through grief. I think we feel reassured that our loved one is close; yet at the same time, we are concerned that this is all a little too weird, like we've been watching too many science fiction movies. We're not socialized to acknowledge or value our encounters with anything unseen, let alone diabetes test strips from the beyond. Yet many believe in heaven, talk freely with angels, search for soul mates, and wait patiently for a miracle. In the field of thanatology, we come across many inexplicable, sometimes mysterious, occurrences associated with dying and grief. It's the mystery of it all that makes some uncomfortable with their experiences. If that is the case for you, talk with a grief counselor to explore what your concerns are and to help you make sense of what is happening. Grief counseling provides a safe, confidential place to share our pain.

I found my unusual experiences comforting. They helped me feel not so alone. And you can bet that I thanked Wally for showing up and saving me from that speeding ticket!

Worksheet VII

Messages?

Write down any unexplainable feelings or experiences about your loved one.

How did it make you feel when it happened?

How do you feel about it now?

In what ways do you continue your relationship with your loved one? How does it help you—or does it not help you?

Epilogue

As most football enthusiasts will tell you, as the season draws to a close, the main question that's asked is, "Is there life after football season?" For some, the answer is not certain. Now, after six years have passed, when I ask myself, "Is there life after Wally?" I can tell you without hesitation that the answer is, "Yes."

Wally and I grew up together; he was my anchor. The life we shared shaped who I am. During times of celebration, such as holidays or anniversaries, the pangs of loss return for a little bit. The sadness accompanying these trips down memory lane is respectfully sentimental, not disturbingly painful. However, the one thing I have noticed is that I do find myself a tad annoyed that Wally is not here to help take in the groceries. Learning to rely on oneself after forty-three years of companionship has its moments. I have not forgotten.

It has taken four years to complete this project of writing my story of the therapeutic value of flower essences and the inner journeys that helped manage my grief. During that time, I have shared the healing values of these therapeutic tools with many clients suffering from loss. Each time, clients report a positive response that helps them to move through loss in a gentler way.

I have come to think of *Moving Through Loss* as a journey from grief to your self. Your wounded self needs you to explore your internal world of feeling, need, and desire. It needs you to shed your tears so that your heart can heal and you can feel wholeness once again. The process will introduce you to your spiritual beliefs in a new and deeper way; it will even help you write your story if you want. And if you will allow, your wounded self will introduce you to your authentic self.

Recovery is not about "just getting used to it." I believe we can do more than that. By living with conscious intention, we can learn from our grief what is important for our well-being. Today I have a greater appreciation for what "living" really means. By doing so, I honor my past, enjoy my present, and embrace my future. I wish you the same.

Resources

Flower essences companies are available throughout the United States and in other countries. Many offer training sessions and workshops and list certified practitioners near you. The following are the ones mentioned in this book.

Bach Flower Essences
Nelson Bach (USA)
21 High Street, Suite 302
North Andover, MA 01845

David Dalton
Delta Gardens
P.O. Box 201
Hampton Falls, NH 03844

Flower Essence Society
Earth-Spirit, Inc.
P.O. Box 459
Nevada City, CA 95959

For those interested in further information on deep imagery:

The International Institute for Visualization Research
www.deepimagery.org/

Academy for Guided Imagery
Admin@AcademyForGuidedImagery.com
Belleruth Naparstek
www.healthjourneys
Resources for Mind, Body & Spirit

C.G.Jung Institute Boston
www.cgjungbost@aol.com

Bibliography

Bach, Edward, MD. *The Bach Flower Remedies.* Revised Edition. New Canaan, CT: Keats, 1997.

Benson, Herbert, MD, et al. *The Wellness Book: The Comprehensive Guide to Maintaining Health and Treating Stress-Related Illness.* Fireside Book, New York: Simon &Schuster, 1992.

Benson, Herbert, MD, et al. *Timeless Healing, The Power and Biology of Belief.* New York: Scribner, 1996.

Dalton, David. *Stars of the Meadow, Medicinal Herbs as Flower Essences.* New York: Steiner Books, 2006.

Doka, Kenneth, PhD. *Disenfranchised Grief, New Directions, Challenges and Strategies for Practice.* Champaign, IL: Research Press, 2002.

Gallegos, Eligio Stephen, PhD. *Animals of the Four Windows, Integrating Thinking, Sensing, Feeling and Imagery.* Santa Fe, NM: Moon Bear Press, 1992.

Gallegos, Eligio Stephen, PhD. *The Personal Totem Pole: Animal Imagery, the Chakras, and Psychotherapy,* 2nd edition. Santa Fe, NM: Moon Bear Press, 1990.

Gerber, Richard, MD. *Vibrational Medicine: The #1 Handbook of Subtle-Energy Therapies.* 3rd edition. Rochester, VT: Bear & Company, 2001.

"Grief Letter." *Transformative Grief-Loss as an Opportunity for Growth.* New England Center for Loss and Transition, Guilford, CT, Vol. II, No.1, Winter, 1996.

Grollman, Earl. *Living When a Loved One Has Died.* 3rd edition. Boston, MA: Beacon Press, 1995.

Hartick, Alice. *Remembrance.* Poems for Modern Youth, Boston, MA: Houghton Mifflin College Division, 1938, p. 397.

Kaminski, Patricia, et al. *Flower Essence Repertory, A Comprehensive Guide to North American and English Flower Essences for Emotional and Spiritual Well-Being.* Nevada City, CA: Flower Essence Society, 1994.

Kast, Verena. *Imagination as Space of Freedom: Dialogue between the Ego and the Unconscious.* New York: International Publishing Corp, 1988.

Naparstek, Belleruth. *Staying Well with Guided Imagery.* New York: Warner Books, 1994.

Worden, J. William. *Grief Counseling & Grief Therapy: A Handbook for the Mental Health Practioner* 2nd edition. New York: Springer Publishing Co., 1991.

About the Authors

Christine L. Bavaro, M.Ed., is a licensed mental health counselor and licensed certified social worker with thirty years of experience counseling individuals, couples and families. A clinical member of the American Association for Marriage and Family Therapy, Chris is a National Certified counselor and a National Board certified diplomate in clinical hypnotherapy. She is trained in mind/body medicine, a certified flower essences practitioner and imagery guide. She is a bereavement group facilitator and holds membership in the American Academy of Bereavement and the Association for Death Education and Counseling. A former adjunct professor at North Shore Community College, she has presented workshops sharing her experience and knowledge with others. Chris has a private practice in Lynnfield, Massachusetts.

Anne Elise O'Connor is an eclectic entrepreneur who wrote and produced an Emmy Award–winning TV series, launched the news department of a TV station in the Cayman Islands, and wrote the life story of a children's action hero. Now, as president of Media Maven Consulting, Anne Elise creates TV programs, keynote presentations, workshops, blogs, and print articles that inspire people to transform their thinking. Her humorous presentations help audiences get past simply surviving a crisis and move on to succeeding—and thriving—in a challenging environment.